WITHDRAWN

How Many Is A Pair?

Ted R. Schaefer

Rourke
Publishing LLC
Vero Beach, Florida 32964

www.rourkepublishing.com

PHOTO CREDITS: © Armentrout: pages 4, 5, 7, 9, 11, 12, 20, 21; © Bradley Mason: page 6; © Rob Friedman: page 10; © Corel: page 13; © Franky DeMeyer: page 14; © Kenn Kiser: page 19

Editor: Robert Stengard-Olliges

Cover design by Nicola Stratford.

Library of Congress Cataloging-in-Publication Data

Schaefer, Ted, 1948-
    How many is a pair? / Ted Schaefer.
        p. cm. -- (My first math 500 Includes index.)
    ISBN 1-59515-976-2 (hardcover)
    ISBN 1-59515-947-9 (paperback)
    1. Binary system (Mathematics)--Juvenile literature. 2.
Counting--Juvenile literature. I. Title.
    QA141.4.S33 2007
    513.2'11--dc22
                                    2006019787

Printed in the USA

CG/CG

Rourke Publishing

www.rourkepublishing.com – sales@rourkepublishing.com
Post Office Box 3328, Vero Beach, FL 32964

Table of Contents

Running Shoes

I am wearing my favorite **pair** of running shoes.

How many is a pair? Count the shoes.

A pair is two.

Today, I race with the twins.

How many people make twins? Count the girls.

Twins are two people.

Tricycles

We race our tricycle.

How many does **tri** mean? Count the wheels?

Tri means three.

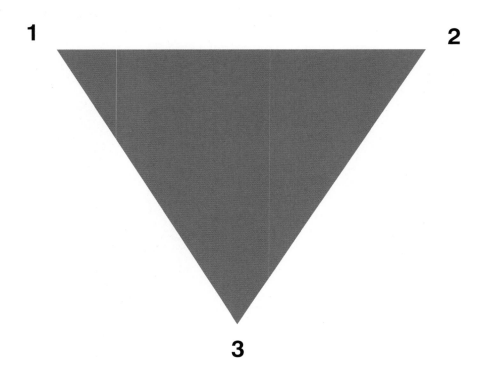

Count and See. If *tri* means three...
then a triangle has three sides

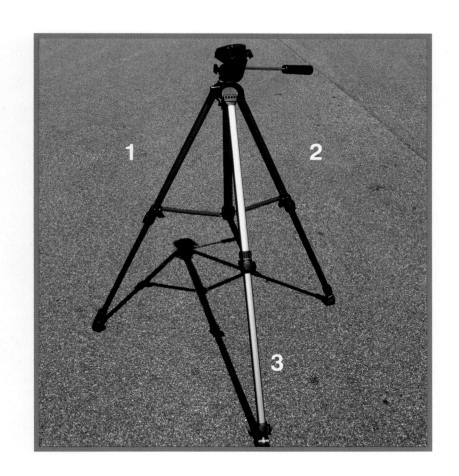

and a tripod has three legs.

We race bicycles.

How many does **bi** mean? Count the wheels.

Bi means two.

Count and See. If *bi* means two…
then binoculars have two tubes

and a biplane has two sets of wings.

A Couple Of Benches

We sit and rest on a **couple** of benches. How many does a "couple" mean? Count the benches.

A couple is two.

A man rides past us on a unicycle. How many does **uni** mean? Count the wheel.

Uni means one.

Count and See. If uni means one...
then music in unison has one sound.

A uniform means everyone wears one kind of clothes.

I sit and rest my pair of tired feet. Aaaaaaah.

Glossary

bi (BYE) — two

couple (KUHP uhl) — two things or people

pair (PAIR) — two of something

tri (TRY) — three

uni (u NEE) — one

Index

Further Reading

Ball, Johnny. *Go Figure!*. DK, 2005.
Glicksman, Caroline. *Eric the Math Bear*. Random House, 2003.
Pistoia, Sara. *Counting*. Child's World*, 2003.

Websites To Visit

pbskids.org/cyberchase/parentsteachers/index.html
www.coolmath-games.com/numbermonster/index.html
www.coolmath4kids.com/coloringbook.html

About The Author

Ted Schaefer is both a writer and a woodworker. When he isn't researching and writing informational books for children, he is building furniture in his shop.